Something Terrible:
A Book of Poetry

Sabrina Andrews

BookLeaf
Publishing

India | USA | UK

Presentation by *BookLeaf Publishing*

Web: www.bookleafpub.com

E-mail: info@bookleafpub.com

ISBN : 9789357447539

First edition 2021

DEDICATION

For my beautiful children - Georgina and Jude.

ACKNOWLEDGEMENT

In what has been one of the hardest years of my life - I wish to thank my family and friends who have been there for me in my darkest moments. You know who you are.

I especially wish to acknowledge my dearest friends Natalie and Amy. Natalie - I'll forever be grateful for you being my wisest friend and my voice of reason; I'm always in admiration of your unfailing strength. And Amy - the kindest person I know. I love you both.

Gun

You did not take aim.
You did not fire the shot.
But you did load the gun.
And I will never forgive you.

Memories

My body is a map of what has happened to me;
the things I cannot remember.
My memories are cracked and broken,
a knot I cannot undo.
When I try to go back
it is blurred and uncertain,
a story with the pages ripped out.
The feelings remain. And the little details.
The paint chips painfully lodged under my
fingernails.
The wallpaper. The view from the window.
The awful things I know, they live under my
skin;
I feel it in my bones, I know it in my soul.
I know what happened.
I live it every day.

Nights - I

I do not now lay awake in the fearful dark
waiting for the shiver of light under the door.
The fateful creak of the floorboards.
My mouth is dry, coated with terror
waiting, waiting, waiting
knowing I am not alone in the night.

I do not fear home.
I do not fear sleep.
I do not fear him.

This was not always true.

A day soon is coming.
We will face each other.
The cold awful truth,
the bottomless, endless horror;
it must be spoken aloud.
It will be ignored no longer.

The reason why

Why did I speak now?

I wanted to.
I was ready to.
Because it wasn't my fault.
Because I deserve justice.
Because the truth should be told.
Because I was a child.
Because I did not ask for it.
Because I will not be silenced.
Because I will not disappear.
Because I will not go away.
Because I will not stop.
Because he cannot win.
Because I never lie.
Because   it   happened.

Because fuck him, that's why.

This is now

Sometimes, I feel so much - so intensely
I cannot unpick the ends or the beginnings.
I sit quietly in the storm of my mind,
the rush of everything

                    and nothing
that I feel.

I'm trying to make sense of this.
I'm trying

        to grab on to something I can hold.

But as I reach out
I feel myself   slipping away

into a time and space long ago.

A pause; a deep breath.
My bare feet on the cold floor.
The lights are dim.
I notice for the first time
the ticking of the kitchen clock

and I say aloud

This is now.
         This is now.
                  This is now.

This is now.

Sometimes I forget.

Anxiety

Everything feels so fucking unbearable.
My skin is crawling, always on the edge of a
knife.
There's a knot in my belly
and my mouth is dry.
My hand shakes when I hold my mug of coffee.
I could cry, but I feel….

nothing.

Something terrible is coming; I feel it in the air.
I am waiting for it, for the moment to come,
but nothing happens.
I spend my time preparing;
I'm ready for anything.
For every implausible situation, they never come
to pass.

I exist in a dangerous world.

You're always just behind me,
never out of my sight.
I find you in the gaze of every man I meet,
lurking

and I wonder
'What do you want from me?'

I hate this.

Anger

Anger is the part of you that knows you are worth being angry about.

The affair

He said
'I've never met anyone like you.'
'I hope I never do again.'
Was it a compliment, or an insult;
I'm still not sure.

It was fun in the beginning.
Drinking and dancing in smoky clubs,
stolen moments and whispered phone calls.
We belonged to the night and banal hotel rooms.

I knew you were not the one for me.
You belonged to someone else.
But I saw something in you; I thought you saw
something in me too.

I was dark and mysterious; at my sultry and
cynical finest,
you were charming and persistent.
I laughed at all of your jokes.
We all fall for this.

     ..... we all fall.

We kept on playing these dangerous games.
Every exchange with you a battle; an endless
fucking war
of sharp words.
Yours sliced through me.
But I always wanted more.
I held on tightly to you,
whilst also knowing a single painful truth:

I cannot do this.

I could feel the ground beneath me shifting,
the brittle foundations of the nothing we were
splintering, cracking, descending.

It ends, of course, it ends.
This ridiculous, clichéd, passionate affair.
One bleak morning;
we have the same old conversation.
I kiss you goodbye,
knowing this will be the last time.
When I tell you, 'I love you',
for the first time, it was a lie.
I walk, keep walking away.

        and I will not come

back.

Leaving

Sometimes words are hard.
Our conversations,
the final one I had with you.
I wish I could forget the look on your face,
every word, a punch in the face.
The dull thud as each word landed a painful
blow.

I'm not proud of what I said.
It hurt me to hurt you.
But I knew too, I could not stay. I could not be.
I had to let it all go and let you go too.

Leaving now, I had to.
Everything we built together,
I ripped it to fucking shreds
and tore it all to pieces.
I stood in the wreckage of our lives
and the sadness and sorrow I inflicted upon you.

I left the life I thought I wanted.
There are no regrets to lament.
I'm not sorry for the time we spent together;
Nor am I sorry for leaving you.

Forever or goodbye

I know I'm not easy
to live with, to be with, to love.
I've been told, over and over.
I know I'm moody and difficult
and I find it hard to tell you
all the important things,
the things I want, the things I need.
And all the things you said you loved about me
are now the things that drive you wild.
You used to seek my gaze in the crowd;
we lived for the moments when our eyes met.
Now you cannot stand the sight of me.
I need you; I always did.
I don't want you to leave.
Can't you stay?
Tell me either way
is this forever, or goodbye.

Desire

How many of the things

                              I want

are also the things I fear and dread?

Something Terrible

I said I was going to write

                    poetry

about you.

Truthfully, I already do.
Over and over,

I love you,
            I love you,
                        I love you.
Painful, pitiful teenage angst
the lyrics to every Smiths song.

My charming man.
What shade of blue are your eyes?
I'm still making up my mind.
It feels like it's only ever been you.

I'm every tired cliché
and all those old love songs;
lines of poetry run through my head.
Everything and nothing, I never get it said.

So yes, my darling, I did try,
to write something that made sense.
To think about you and write something
beautiful;
I picked up my pen and poured out something
terrible instead.

Insomnia

It's so late.
I can't sleep.
I shut my eyes and I think about you.

The way you look when you smile.
The way your eyes sparkle,
when you tell me a joke.
My hands know your body,
the way you feel under me
and my hand fits in yours.
You pull me in to be close to you
I rest my head on your chest
your arm wrapped around me.
You sigh and I close my eyes,
I pull the blankets over us.
We sit this way, quietly, contentedly.

This is what I think of, when I can't sleep.
The way you look at me, whenever we meet.
And you telling me, a simple, undisputable truth,
one that even I cannot deny,
'I love you.'

We must die now

The worst part of me
whispers and softly tells me
that I cannot
have these beautiful moments with you.

I must destroy you.
We must die now, while there is still time.

A beautiful view

Today we walked along the beach;
a beautiful autumn afternoon.
Bathed in my favourite sound, the rushing waves
and the sun shone.
Hand in hand,
we stopped and paused to admire the view.
You looked at the sea;

I looked at you.

Forever

We sat together on my sofa.
You lay against me, your back to my chest;
I wrapped my arms around you.
You held my hand and gently squeezed,
we sat together in contented silence.
And as I softly kissed your cheek
I wished only that I would remember this
moment

                                        And keep it

forever.

Freedom

Freedom can be a lonely place.
But I would rather be alone
than die of unhappiness.

Relentless

There is something inside of me

                      that will not

surrender,

                      will not give

up,

                      will not stop.

This part of me persists, always
in the face of adversity, sorrow, pain
and all those who attempt to oppress me.

No matter how much I am   pushed
                                 pulled
                                 when I am
toppled by you

I must rise; I go on regardless.
I am relentless.

Alive

I will never apologise for finding myself alive
under the weight of everyone else's
expectations.

This life is mine and goddamn it, I want all of it.
I want every joy-filled, heart-wrenching,
heart-breaking, heart-bursting, drunken-dancing,
cackling-laughter,
I-can't-believe-this-bullshit-is-happening-to-me
moment.

I want everything.

Nights - II

My favourite nights are the ones when
I'm curled up in bed alone.
A breeze blows in through the open window
the flutter of the curtains
and the silver moonlight illuminates the room.
The sound of rain falling
and nearby an owl hoots.
My cat stirs, purrs, asleep on the bed.
Next door, my children sleep peacefully,
soundly, deeply, dreaming.
Safely.
This little house, my favourite place,
everything I ever dreamed of.